Influence Equation

Unlocking the True Potential of Communication

Table of Contents

Chapter 1. Introduction

In the dynamic world of today, effective communication has never held more power or promise. With the dawn of the digital age, the interaction landscape has been reshaped dramatically, necessitating a reconfiguration of the way we talk, listen and connect. Our Special Report on the 'Influence Equation: Unlocking the True Potential of Communication' presents an engaging and enlightening exploration of this crucial subject. You're invited to dive deep into the heart of communication science and unlock the door to endless possibilities, all crafted in a context that guarantees simplicity and pleasure. Willing to master the subtleties of influence, power, and communication? Let this report be your compass, guiding you on a journey wherein every word, gesture, and silence truly matters, and each conversation holds the potential to be a game-changer. Buy this special report now and shape your communication into your most influential tool!

Chapter 2. Demystifying the Influence Equation

In diving headlong into the world of communication science, the first step will be untangling the concept of the influence equation. An understanding of this equation marks the beginning of a process that promises to refine and revolutionize your communication. By understanding the variables involved in this composition and their interplay, you can unlock a transformative new perspective on your interaction framework.

2.1. Understanding the Influence Equation

To demystify the influence equation, let's first establish what influence truly represents. Influence can be understood as the capacity to affect the character, development, or behavior of someone or something, or the effect itself. In the context of communication, it is the power to cause changes without directly forcing them to happen. The influence equation is a conceptual construct that explains the factors that contribute to this capacity.

This equation suggests that Influence (I) = Authority (A) x Trust (T) x Empathy (E) x Knowledge (K). Here, the Authority represents the weight of your words, the Trust shows the faith others place in you, Empathy refers to your ability to understand others' emotions, and Knowledge speaks of your wisdom and information pool. Each of these factors has its part to play, and excelling in one invariably requires performing well in the others.

2.2. Authority (A)

Authority, within the influence equation, refers to the perceived power or credibility that an individual has. This power can be obtained through various sources - expertise, position, reputation, etc. The greater your authority, the more likely people are to heed your words.

At its core, the communication authority carries a dual responsibility: being knowledgeable enough to command respect and also being proficient enough to convey information effectively. This includes evoking accurate resonance, maintaining transparency, and ensuring the overall quality of information.

2.3. Trust (T)

Trust can be seen as the very foundation upon which any communication rests. It involves a certain faith, confidence, or assurance that the person can be relied upon. The trust factor impacts not only the acceptance of what is communicated but also the way it is received and perceived.

Trust is not handed over; it is earned. And it is earned not just by voicing right things but also by demonstrating consistency in actions, maintaining credibility, ensuring reliability, and confirming predictability. As a communicator, building trust is about fostering relationships based on integrity, honesty, and consistency.

2.4. Empathy (E)

Empathy may seem like an odd inclusion in what might be considered quite a logical and objective equation. Nonetheless, empathy is a crucial part of impactful communication. It refers to understanding others' feelings - not sympathizing or feeling sorry for them, but genuinely grasping their perspective.

Empathy comes into play during communication as deeper understanding, active listening, openness, and even as emotional intelligence. It allows a communicative relation where emotions and body language are understood just as words. When people feel truly understood, it engenders a higher level of trust, opens the door to better relationships and increases the probability of your influence.

2.5. Knowledge (K)

Knowledge is the foundation of any authoritative standpoint. This could take the form of understanding, awareness, or familiarity gained by experience or learning. Knowledge translates into compelling arguments, well-informed opinions, and holistic perspective, thereby making your communication more impactful.

The notion of knowledge is twofold. Firstly, it is about individual depth, i.e., personal experience, gained expertise, and understanding in a particular field. Secondly, it also emphasizes the breadth, indicating how far one can integrate and understand concepts from other related (or even unrelated) domains to bring a richer context.

2.6. Balancing the Equation

While all factors are integral to the equation, attaining a balanced mixture is what molds effective communication. An imbalance can significantly diminish your influential capacity. For example, an extensive knowledge base can register as authoritative but may falter without empathy or trust.

Thus, an efficient influencer recognizes the dynamics of these variables, strives for balance, and adjusts according to situation, context, and audience. It further involves retaining a learning mindset, cultivating emotional intelligence, establishing credibility, and working to expand knowledge.

2.7. The Journey Forward

The path to mastering the influence equation isn't a destination but a journey. It involves learning, application, reflection, and improvement. It's a consistent honing of skills across multiple dimensions and understanding that each interaction is a chance to learn and grow, thereby progressively enhancing your influential capacity.

This report presents an opportunity to dig deeper into each variable of the Influence Equation, uncover its intricate components, and learn the art of wielding them to maximize their potential. This journey is about evolving from a communicator to an influencer - solidifying your Authority, building unshakeable Trust, nurturing deep-seated Empathy, and expanding all-encompassing Knowledge.

In the following chapter, we'll begin this immersive journey by exploring Authority, breaking it down to understand its components, and devising techniques to strengthen its presence.

(end of chapter)

Chapter 3. Understanding the Fundamentals of Communication

Communication, widely understood as the exchange of ideas, thoughts, emotions, and information, is the very backbone of human relationships. These interactions take place through various forms, including speech, writing, signs, symbols, body language, or even silence. Understanding its fundamentals not only enhances our personal and professional interactions but also enriches our perception of the world around us.

3.1. The Context of Communication

It is essential to understand that communication does not occur in a vacuum. It is an intricate process that works within a particular context, which encapsulates several facets. These include the relationship and history between the communicators, the environment, cultural practices, the intent of the message, and the mode of communication. For instance, the tone and context in which we address our colleagues during a professional meeting will differ significantly from how we communicate with friends at a party. These details are based on our understanding of the situation, setting, and relationships. Recognizing the context helps to ensure that our messages are conveyed appropriately and effectively with the desired impact.

3.2. Verbal and Non-Verbal Communication

There are two main types of communication: verbal communication, which uses words, and non-verbal communication, which utilizes body language, tone of voice, facial expressions, gestures, and silence. Both types play crucial roles in conveying our messages. For example, words can express our thoughts and ideas, while our body language and tone can provide further nuance and context.

Verbal communication, which includes both spoken and written words, is the most direct form of sharing our thoughts or ideas. It is what we typically think of when we talk about communication. It allows us to articulate complex concepts, ask questions, provide answers, and create narratives. However, it is susceptible to misinterpretation and misunderstanding if the words are not carefully chosen or the context is not adequately understood.

Non-verbal communication is often more subtle but just as influential. It includes visual cues, body language, tone of voice, personal space, touch, and even the use of silence. While elements like facial expressions and postures can reinforce or contradict the verbal communication, tones and silences can effectively express emotions or create emphasis. For example, a firm tone of voice can convey authority, whereas silence can signify agreement, disagreement, comfort, or even tension.

3.3. The Process of Communication

Successful communication is a process involving several steps. First, the sender conceives an idea or message. This idea is then encoded into a suitable medium (words, symbols, gestures, etc.) and transmitted through a suitable channel (speech, writing, sign language, etc.). The receiver then decodes the message, interpreting its meaning and responding accordingly, thus providing feedback to the sender. This exchange continues back and forth, creating a constant cycle of encoding, transmitting, decoding, and responding.

Each stage of this process can impact the effectiveness of the communication. For instance, the choice of encoding, the clarity of the transmission, the receiver's ability to decode correctly, and the appropriateness of the response can all help make communication successful or lead to misunderstandings.

3.4. Barriers to Effective Communication

Though effective communication may seem straightforward, numerous barriers can hinder its success. These can range from language differences, cultural misunderstandings, and emotional biases to physical distractions, information overload, or simply a poor choice of communication channel. Overcoming these barriers often requires patience, empathy, and — most significantly — an awareness of their existence and impact.

For example, language barriers may lead to misunderstanding if the communicator and the receiver do not share the same language or if the communicator uses jargon or terms unfamiliar to the receiver. Similarly, cultural differences may result in misunderstanding if the communicators have different norms, practices, or interpretations of certain words, gestures, or symbols. Emotional biases can also distort communication; a listener might selectively hear or misunderstand messages based on their preconceptions or emotional state. An awareness of these and other barriers can assist in navigating communication challenges more successfully.

3.5. Communication, Influence, and Power

Understanding the fundamentals of communication is not just about exchanging information—it also encompasses how communication can influence thoughts, attitudes, and actions. The use of persuasive language, authoritative tone, and compelling body language can dramatically impact one's ability to sway an audience. Moreover, non-verbal cues can often speak louder than words, connecting at deeper levels and triggering emotions, interests, and connections based on this 'hidden communication.'

In the realm of communication, knowledge truly is power: the power to influence, to inform, to inspire, and to drive change. Using communication effectively can enable us to convince others of our ideas, gain support for our causes, and establish robust professional relationships.

In this constant progression and evolution of communication practices, we must strive to not only comprehend its roots and basics but continually adapt and evolve with it. Acknowledge it, harness it, and let this intangible asset become one of your strongest tools, distinguishing you in whatever path you choose to tread.

3.6. Concluding Thoughts

In sum, communication is an essential aspect of human existence — a complex, multi-faceted process that involves more than just exchanging words. It encapsulates our history, relationships, culture, and emotions. Recognizing the context, understanding verbal and non-verbal cues, grasping the process, acknowledging the barriers, and realizing its power are fundamental to developing effective communication skills. So, as we continue to use communication as our primary tool for connecting with the world, let's strive to comprehend, improve, and master it one conversation at a time.

Chapter 4. Tuning into the Frequency of Empathy

Consider empathy as a specific frequency - a wavelength that individuals must tune into to fully comprehend the emotions and perspectives of others. This chapter delves into the intricacies of empathy and directs the reader on how to adjust their cognitive radios and tune into this life-altering frequency.

4.1. The Essence of Empathy

Empathy, in its purest form, is the ability to understand and share another person's emotions and experiences as if they were your own. It involves stepping into someone else's shoes, viewing the world through their lens, and genuinely feeling their joy, their pain, their confusion, and their triumphs. By honing your empathy, you can create a profound, meaningful connection with others that transcends mere sympathy and paves the way for effective, influential communication.

4.2. Underlying Mechanics of Empathy

Empathy doesn't simply emerge out of thin air – it is backed by interesting neuroscience. Neuroscientists refer to 'mirror neurons' – a set of neurons that fire both when a person performs an action and when they see someone else perform the same action. This mechanism enables us to mirror the emotions of others, fostering empathy.

The act of empathy also stimulates the release of oxytocin, often referred to as the 'bonding hormone.' This neurochemical facilitates trust, rapport, and warmth between individuals, reinforcing empathetic behavior and promoting stronger, healthier relationships.

4.3. The Empathy Spectrum

Empathy finds expression in three main forms: cognitive empathy, emotional empathy, and compassionate empathy.

Cognitive empathy refers to understanding what another person is feeling and being able to perceive their viewpoint. Essentially, it's about thought more than feeling. One can show cognitive empathy by paraphrasing a person's feelings or summarising their experiences, showing they understand.

Emotional empathy, on the other hand, is feeling what another person is feeling. From an evolutionary standpoint, this could be the primitive form of empathy that allowed early humans to respond to the emotions and needs of their kin, thereby promoting survival.

Lastly, compassionate empathy combines both understanding and feeling with the drive to help if needed. This type of empathy doesn't just infer understanding or mirror feelings but also motivates us to take action.

Each of these types of empathy serves a useful purpose and may be more or less appropriate depending on the situation. Mastering when and how to use each type can significantly enhance communication.

4.4. The Power of Empathetic Communication

Empathy doesn't just benefit the recipient – the person offering empathy stands to gain significantly as well. The ability to empathize fosters trust and rapport, which are the bedrock of any successful interaction. When people feel heard and understood, they are more open to your ideas, making your communication effective and influential.

Awareness is the first step towards cultivating empathy. It requires anticipation, focused attention, and active listening. By carefully observing others' body language, facial expressions, and words, we can tune into their underlying emotions and perspectives.

Practice becomes key in honing empathetic communication. It means continuously reminding oneself to evaluate others' feelings, wants, and needs in communication, placing their feelings as a priority and responding in a way that validates these emotions.

4.5. The Art of Listening in Empathy

Effective listening is one of the cornerstones of empathy. It helps us understand the emotions and perspectives of others. Active listening requires our full attention and an open mind. It involves verbally and nonverbally responding to the speaker, validating their feelings and viewpoints, and encouraging further communication.

4.6. Overcoming the Empathy Gap

At times, empathy may not come easily. This is known as an empathy gap. Overcoming it requires conscious effort. Start with self-awareness and understanding your own emotions. This self-exploration also involves recognizing your biases and prejudices and acknowledging and overcoming them. Then, try to perceive the world from the other person's view, keeping an open mind. This empathetic exercise helps bring humans closer and communicate more effectively, bridging the seemingly impassable empathy gap.

4.7. Empathy: A Choice and Skill

Empathy is more than just a trait; it's a skill to be nurtured. Like any skill, it can be mastered through deliberate practice and constant learning. It's also a choice one makes every day - to connect or disconnect, to understand or to ignore, to reach out or to remain indifferent.

Empathy in communication is not about solving problems or making pain disappear; it's about understanding and reinforcing the fact that no one is alone in their experiences. As we learn to tune into this frequency of empathy, we can unlock the true potential of communication, paving the way for deeper connections and positive change.

Chapter 5. Optimizing Verbal and Non-Verbal Cues

In the realm of effective communication, both verbal and non-verbal cues play a crucial role. These cues, when used optimally, contribute to ensuring your message is comprehended correctly in its entirety. In this section, you will learn how to optimize your verbal and non-verbal cues to enhance your communication skills.

5.1. Understanding Verbal Cues

Verbal cues refer to signals conveyed through the words we use, tone, inflection or other elements of speech. They can be intentional or unintentional, and can often convey more about a message than the words themselves.

1. **Choice of Words**: The selection of words is of paramount importance in communication. Words that are easy to understand and appropriate to the context ensure that the listener comprehends the intended message.

2. **Tone and Inflection**: The way spoken words are articulated delivers important cues. A change in tone or inflection can completely modify the meaning of a sentence. Therefore, it is crucial to match tone with the intended message.

3. **Pace of Speech**: Speech speed can signal confidence, anxiety, or contemplation. Too fast might indicate nervousness, while slow might hint thoughtful deliberations. The right pace is crucial to communicating effectively.

4. **Pause**: Intelligent use of silence can be powerful. It can indicate a shift in topics, provide listeners a breather, or emphasize a particular point.

To optimize verbal cues, consider the four elements mentioned above. Watch your words, set the right tone, adjust your pace, and use the tactical pause to enhance their effect.

5.2. The Power of Non-Verbal Cues

Non-verbal cues involve signals conveyed through means other than words, such as body language, facial expressions, gestures, and posture, among others. These cues can often communicate more than the spoken words themselves.

1. **Body Language**: Body language is an important communicator. Open or closed postures, folded or open arms, leaning forward or backward, can all communicate different messages. An open posture generally signifies positivity and acceptance.

2. **Facial Expressions**: Our face is perhaps the most expressive part of our body and can easily betray our emotions. Smiles, frowns, surprise, disgust, etc. are all conveyed through our face. A genuine smile can ease any tension, while a frown can communicate disapproval.

3. **Eye Contact**: Maintaining eye contact is crucial. It communicates confidence and establishes a connection with the listener. But it should be balanced, as excessive eye contact can make the other person uncomfortable.

4. **Gestures**: Hand and arm movements augment verbal communication. They not only help illustrate what you're saying but also display your enthusiasm and involvement in the conversation.

5. **Proximity**: The distance between speakers can indicate the level of comfort or the nature of the relationship. Respect personal space, yet do not create an uncomfortable distance.

In order to optimize non-verbal cues, pay attention to these aspects. Stay aware of your body language, observe others' reactions, and adjust your approach accordingly.

5.3. Managing Paralanguage

Paralanguage refers to vocal communication that is separate from actual language. This includes factors such as tone of voice, loudness, inflection, and pitch. Sarcasm, enthusiasm, anger, or surprise are all conveyed through paralanguage. Understanding and managing your paralanguage effectively is a vital part of optimizing verbal and non-verbal cues.

5.4. Enhancing Active Listening

While we often focus on our speaking skills, listening is equally important. Active listening involves fully concentrating, understanding, responding, and then remembering what is being said. Nodding in agreement, maintaining eye contact, or echoing the speaker's sentiments are all part of active listening skills. Developing the art of active listening enables us to better respond and engage in conversations.

The full potential of communication doesn't solely stem from what you say, but how you say it. Therefore, enhancing and managing verbal and non-verbal cues indeed serve as integral steps towards better personal and professional interactions.

Chapter 6. Power of Silence: The Art of Strategic Pauses

In an era of information overload, where words are in surplus and incessant chatter often overwhelms, there's a markedly underappreciated element of communication resurfacing with unique strength and influence - silence. Far from being a communication break, silence offers a multifaceted tool to wield influence, harness power, and shape conversations. Strategic pauses, in particular, profoundly affect the rhythm and tempo of discussions, permeate beyond surface-level talk, and foster deeper connections.

6.1. Understanding Silence and its Impact

Defining silence is more complex than it initially appears. Predominantly, it refers to the absence of sound, the non-verbal, or the void between words and sentences. However, scholars have evolved this definition to include "communicative silence," which emphasizes intentional and constructive silence. It is not a mere absence, but an active force carrying its own meaning.

Communicative silence is no stranger to us. We employ it daily in various forms: allowing a friend to pour out their emotions uninterrupted, patiently waiting for a child to form a response, or providing space after a rhetorical question for dramatic effect. Strategic pauses are all indications of communicative silence.

But why is silence impactful? The reason lies in its duality. It's both a reflection and an influencer of emotion. An uneasy silence can magnify tension, while a compassionate silence can console. It adds depth to verbal communication and carries the power to transform the narrative.

6.2. The Art of Strategic Pauses

Strategic pauses can influence communication remarkably. The effectiveness of these pauses, however, often depends on mastering four essential aspects: timing, duration, context, and reception.

The timing of a pause can decide its impact. For instance, easy-to-miss nuances in spoken language are emphasized when followed by a pause, drawing attention to the importance of the information.

Duration plays a role too, with longer pauses often resounding more than shorter ones. This isn't always beneficial; an elongated silence may convey awkwardness or hostility instead of thoughtfulness or respect.

Context decides if a pause will prosper or falter. A pause in a debate may symbolize a lost argument, while the same pause in a therapy session might provide much-needed breathing room.

Lastly, how the receiving party interprets the silence is critical. Variations might stem from cultural, social, or individual differences—every person perceives silence in their unique way.

6.3. Applying Strategic Pauses

To wield the power of silence, let's look at few areas application: leadership, presentations, negotiations, and personal growth.

In leadership, a pause can transmit authority, affording leaders a moment to collect their thoughts, thus projecting confidence and control. Pauses contribute to careful decision making, projecting a thoughtful leadership style that invites trust and respect.

Presentations can benefit tremendously from well-placed pauses. They provide listeners a fleeting moment to absorb complex information, contribute to pacing the talk, add dramatic effect, and energize the presenter-audience connection.

Negotiations are another arena where strategic pauses can be advantageous. They allow space for the other party to clarify their thoughts, take a breather during intense conversations or to show respect by listening actively. They also strategically let the negotiator create anticipation or discomfort to elicit more information from the opponent.

In terms of personal growth, silence offers a sanctuary for introspection. Pauses empower people to evaluate their emotions and thoughts, fostering emotional intelligence and empathy—critical parts of effective communication.

It is vital, though, to remember that silence, like any tool, can be misused. Cultivating the power of silence is about understanding the subtle balance between speaking and not speaking, taking action and refraining, making noise, or enveloping oneself in quiet. Fail to strike this balance, and silence can quickly slip into avoidance, concealment, or passivity.

6.4. Conclusion

In the full orchestra of communication, silence and strategic pauses are the subtle notes often missed. Yet they carry a remarkable potential to reshape the dynamics of a conversation, wield power, and incite influence.

Training oneself in the art of strategic silence is not about suppression of voice; rather, it reflects an appreciation of the rhythm and music in conversation. It is about providing necessary breathing spaces to amplify the significance of words, foster connections, and facilitate understanding. Perhaps it's time we stop viewing silence as a conversation's empty spaces and start acknowledging it as an irreplaceable part of the influential communication puzzle.

Chapter 7. Active Listening: Not Just Hearing, but Understanding

In the realm of communication, what often slips through the cracks is our ability to actively *listen*. Lending your ears to someone doesn't merely imply hearing their words. True power lies in comprehension, interpretation, and response.

Active listening is a skill that, when honed, can lead to not only a deeper understanding of the people around you, but also improved relationships, clearer communication, and increased influence.

7.1. The Art and Science of Active Listening

Scientifically speaking, active listening provides an advantage as it employs the highest form of cognitive processing. This engagement goes beyond the physiological act of hearing and enters the domain of decoding, understanding, and responding to the conveyed information.

The art of active listening dwells in the realm of empathy and mindfulness. As an active listener, you are not merely absorbing words; you're acknowledging emotions, interpreting tone, and respecting the speaker's perspective. Crucially, you are creating a safe, non-judgemental space that promotes open dialogue and mutual respect.

7.2. The Four Pillars of Active Listening

Active listening stands on four pivotal pillars:

1. Attention

2. Interpretation

3. Responding

4. Recalling

Paying *attention* signifies your willingness to listen, denoting respect for the speaker. This mindfulness not only involves hearing the words but also noticing non-verbal cues, such as facial expressions, body language, and tone of voice.

Interpretation is the phase where you decipher the conveyed messages, accounting for the cultural, organizational, or personal contexts that often subtly influence communications. A skilled interpreter discerns the nuanced meanings that blanket the said words.

Responding takes active listening from a passive to an interactive process. Your responses, shaped by the extent and precision of your understanding, should echo in sync with the speaker's perspective.

Lastly, *recalling* showcases your understanding as you remember and reference key points from the conversation. This ability not only proves that you were engaged in the conversation, but also that you value what the speaker shared.

7.3. The Role of Physiology in Active Listening

Physiological factors greatly affect listening skills. Eye contact, nodding, and mirroring are non-verbal behaviors that signify active-engagement. A relaxed posture, steady gaze, and oral paraphrasing communicate interest, showing that the speaker's thoughts, feelings, and perspectives matter to you. By 'leaning in' physically, we also 'lean in' psychologically.

7.4. Active Listening in the Digital Age

Active listening extends beyond face-to-face dialogue. In the era of virtual communication, we must navigate new challenges to ensure effective active listening. With the current trend towards digital interactions, the conventional tactics of eye contact, body language, and non-verbal cues are often lost. Pay close attention to the 'tone' of written messages while respecting and responding to the intended sentiment. Additionally, during video calls, maintaining 'eye contact' with the camera or maintaining a composed demeanor can signal your active participation.

7.5. The Influence of Active Listening

Active listening plays a critical role in molding you as an 'influencer'. It fosters empathy and understanding, imparting a sense of value to the speaker. When people feel heard, they feel respected and are likely to reciprocate the same level of respect.

Moreover, active listeners cultivate a clear and comprehensive grasp of problems due to their aptitude for detecting nuances. This in-depth understanding allows them to chart evidence-based, well-informed solutions.

As boundaries dissolve in the digital age, becoming an active listener opens up doors towards cross-cultural understanding and global empathy - prerequisites for any influential communicator.

In summary, active listening, with its multi-pronged facets, stands at the heart of every conversation. Every spoken word, unspoken emotion, hidden intent, and noticeable reaction carries meaning; it will only resonate if one listens, processes, and comprehends actively. So, let's arm ourselves with attention, empathy, patience, and genuine curiosity, and ascend to a higher level of communication and influence. We must remember that not only does every voice deserve to be heard, but more importantly, understood.

Chapter 8. Crafting Messages that Resonate

Understanding the power of communication requires not only the realization of the importance of our words but of the messages they deliver. To be influential communicators, we need to create messages that resonate deeply within those who receive them. Resonant messages can ignite emotion, trigger action, and even inspire a revolution. To do this, we need to delve into the intricacies of shaping such messages.

8.1. The Core of Resonant Messages

A resonant message reverberates in the minds of your audience. At the core of these messages lies the delicate blend of substance, relatability, and emotion. The substance is the core informational content of the message. Relatability is the ability of that substance to connect with the listener or reader at a deeper level. Finally, the emotion decides how it makes your audience feel. Together, they form a cocktail that edifies the listeners, thereby ensuring message resonance.

8.2. Crafting Substance in Messages

The true power of your message lies in the heart of what you say - the substance. An influential message needs a robust substance, which can be achieved by:

- **Research:** Before crafting the message, undertake a comprehensive investigation about the topic, the audience, and the platform. This research may involve exploring past communications, understanding audience demographics, and foreseeing potential reactions.

- **Structure:** A well-organized structure forms the backbone of your substance. It results in the clear and coherent delivery of thoughts. Mainly, this involves being precise with your introduction, middle, and conclusion.

- **Content:** The content should be clear, compelling, and engaging. It must fit reader expectations and provide value. A balance between novelty and familiarity will keep your audience engaged.

8.3. Making Messages Relatable

The second ingredient of a resonant message is relatability. Here's how you can incorporate it into your messages:

- **Empathy:** Understand your audience's needs, wants, and desires. Speak their language and build your messages around the problems they encounter and the solutions they seek.

- **Personalization:** A personalized touch with the use of direct speech, anecdotes, or scenarios helps in creating a connection with your audience. They must feel that the message is specifically meant for them.

- **Contextualization:** Context enhances clarity. Incorporate relevant data, quotes, examples, or images to give context to your claims. This will help the audience to relate your message with everyday life and experiences.

8.4. Instigating Emotion

No message resonates unless it tugs at the heartstrings. Here's how to instigate emotion:

- **Storytelling:** Represent your message as a narrative with flesh-and-blood characters, a plot, and a conflict. Storytelling brings in an emotional depth that makes it easier to grasp and remember messages.

- **Powerful Imagery:** Deploying metaphors, analogies or vivid descriptions creates stark mental images, intensifying the message's emotional impact.

- **Call to Action:** By asking your audience to take action, you not only create involvement, but also generate a sense of urgency and motivation.

8.5. Effective Delivery

With the message crafted, it is time to consider its delivery. Concentrate on:

- **Pace:** Speak clearly and at an easy-to-follow pace. Too fast and your audience may miss important points. Too slow and they may lose interest.

- **Pitch and Tone:** Maintain a moderate and consistent pitch and tone. Avoid ups and downs that might make the message difficult to understand.

- **Body Language:** Ensure that your non-verbal cues align with your verbal ones. Body language can add to or detract from your message.

By considering these factors, we can craft resonant messages that influence, inspire, and motivate. Remember, every word counts in the grand narrative; every sentence is a brushstroke on the canvas of understanding. Create your masterpiece, and let your communication resonate.

Chapter 9. Influence and Digital Communication: The New Frontier

With the advent of the digital age, influence has acquired a new frontier: digital communication. This is a sphere that holds infinite potential but also presents both exceptional opportunities and daunting challenges, raising questions about power dynamics, interpersonal relations, the protection of privacy, and the fine line dividing influence from manipulation. The reliance on digital platforms has further complicated the communication spectrum, demanding heightened awareness, skill, and adaptability to maximize influence effectively.

9.1. The Emergence of the Digital Age

The roots of the digital age sprouted with the introduction of the Internet in the late 20th century and gradually bloomed with the evolution of digital devices and networking platforms. As we entered the 21st century, rapid technological advancements boosted the capabilities of the Internet, fostering connections that weren't possible before.

The digital age generated an environment where communication extended beyond physical proximity, enabling real-time conversations despite geographical constraints and time zones. With boosted communication channels, the art of influence also shifted its terrain. Able to speak to a global audience instantaneously, the potential for influence skyrocketed.

9.2. The Power of Digital Communication

The crux of using digital communication lies in its far-reaching connectivity. Businesses, for instance, are no longer limited by location. They can approach a global audience, target demographics according to their preferences, and retain a strong brand presence online. Digital communication amplifies a company's voice, enhancing their influence on a broader scale.

Digital platforms also provide a safe space for individuals to express their opinions, fostering a vibrant and diverse global community that gains its power from the collective contribution. Yet, the freedom of expression is not without its intricacies. With the heightened voices, listening becomes a critical skill. Influencers must learn to filter relevant from irrelevant noise and harness effective strategies to keep their audience engaged.

9.3. The Essentials of Digital Influence

Influence in the digital world isn't just about your digital footprint; it is a complex blend of credibility, engagement, and the capacity to inspire action. At its core, digital influence is not limited to the number of followers or likes one has—it encompasses the power to leave an impact, to change perspectives, to shape decisions and trends.

To harness the power of digital influence, one must establish a strong and reputable online presence and engage with their community. Additionally, content plays a pivotal role; it should be original, compelling, and add value to the lives of the audience. In addition, influencers must be open to two-way communication, understanding their audience's needs and creating space for them to express their opinions.

9.4. The Ethical Implications of Digital Influence

With great power comes great responsibility; the digital space is no exception to this rule. As users of digital platforms continue to grow exponentially, so do concerns about ethical issues relating to privacy, behavior, and disclosure.

In today's world, data is a powerful tool. While it can be used to understand the needs and preferences of consumers, it can also be manipulated to skew perspectives and influence decisions. Therefore, ethical considerations must take center stage in any discussion on digital influence. Utilizing influence responsibly involves transparency, respecting audiences' right to privacy, and curbing disinformation.

9.5. Navigating Potential Challenges

The digital world is constantly evolving, and with it, the challenges of digital communication. Cyberbullying, misinformation, and the spread of hate speech have ramped up with digital communication's widespread use. These issues not only raise ethical concerns but also impact the overall essence of communication, making it imperative to tackle them judiciously.

Digital literacy is crucial in navigating these challenges, including understanding the implications of digital footprints, ensuring data privacy, and discerning credible from unreliable sources.

Influence in the digital world has the potential to transform societies and break down barriers. However, it must be used sustainably and ethically to serve best the shifting landscape of communication. Having a comprehensive understanding of digital communication's essence is the first step towards unlocking the true potential of influence. A not so distant future could have us witnessing every person, each conversation, indeed, every silence, as an opportunity to engage, inspire, and induce meaningful action—a level of influence that truly refines the art of communication.

Chapter 10. Dealing with Communication Barriers and Misunderstandings

Dealing with communication barriers and misunderstandings involves a rigorous understanding of their origins and the effective techniques needed to overcome them. Modern communication may boast high speed and broad reach, but it's also rife with hurdles that can distort the intended messages and mar the process with inefficiencies. Let's start our dive into this subject by focusing on the major communication barriers that often come into play.

10.1. Identification and Understanding of Communication Barriers

Barriers in communication can be the result of numerous factors, be they physical, psychological, or cultural, each with their specific challenges and solutions.

Physical Barriers

A physical barrier could be as straightforward as distance between individuals, background noise, poor quality equipment, or even time zone differences. These obstacles often lead to the misinterpretation of signals or complete communication breakdowns.

Psychological Barriers

These encompass factors like stress, emotions, perceptions, preconceived notions, and biases, which can affect the way people perceive and interpret messages. Mental health is an understated barrier that can significantly affect communication, causing misunderstandings or conflicts.

Cultural Barriers

Owing to globalization, communication across cultural boundaries has never been more prevalent. Thus, cultural barriers, such as different languages, customs, beliefs, or values, tend to create misunderstandings and can cause messages to be lost in translation.

Once identified, pinpointing these barriers is the first step to dealing with them. Now, let's delve into strategies to overcome these barriers.

10.2. Tactics to Overcome Physical Barriers

Tackling physical barriers requires practical and technical solutions. Investments in high-quality communication technology and understanding the best times and venues for communication can mitigate these issues significantly.

- Impeccable Technology: Ensure good quality, accessible, and reliable communication equipment. Regular testing and maintenance can prevent equipment failure.

- Optimal Time and Space: Schedule conversations or meetings at times and places that are mutually convenient and free of interruptions.

10.3. Strategies to Overcome Psychological Barriers

Addressing psychological barriers is a more delicate process. It involves creating a safe, accepting space for communication where empathy and active listening govern.

- Be Empathetic: Try to understand and consider the emotions and feelings of others.

- Active Listening: Listen to understand, not just respond. Acknowledge the other person's perspectives.

10.4. Techniques to Overcome Cultural Barriers

Cultural competency is required to understand and respect the diverse cultures you interact with. Breaking the barriers involves educating oneself about different cultures, avoiding ethnocentrism, and choosing simplicity in communication.

- Cultivate Cultural Awareness: Understanding cultural contexts can help pave the way for successful communication across boundaries.

- Simplify Your Message: Avoid culture-specific idioms, slang, or jargon that may not translate well. Stick with clear, simple language.

From here, let's further discuss the dealing with misunderstandings, another aspect critical to successful communication.

10.5. Understanding and Addressing Misunderstandings

Misunderstandings are common in professional as well as personal communication, often leading to unnecessary conflicts. The keys to managing them are awareness, clarity, patience, and a non-accusatory approach.

- Clarity and Confirmation: Make sure to articulate your message clearly and confirm it has been correctly understood.

- Patience and Composure: Be patient, listen attentively, and maintain composure while dealing with misunderstandings.

- Open-Mindedness: Encourage an environment where all parties feel free to express themselves without fear of judgement.

10.6. Conflicts from Misunderstandings: Prevention and Resolution

Preventing conflicts from misunderstandings is strongly preferable to resolving them. However, when conflicts do arise, they must be managed effectively.

- Preventing Conflicts: Ensure that the communication process is open, clear, and inclusive, which reduces chances of misunderstandings.

- Conflict Resolution: Understand the root cause of the conflict, empathize with others' perspectives and negotiate a mutually acceptable solution.

In conclusion, overcoming communication barriers and misunderstanding requires a multifaceted approach, honed through awareness, understanding, and practice. With a solid understanding of these concepts, you'll be better equipped to navigate the intricate landscape of effective communication.

Chapter 11. Cementing Influence: Building Sustained, Meaningful Connections

Influence: it's not a transaction, but rather a relationship built on trust and consistent communication. If done right, this relationship paves the way for sustained, meaningful connections. This chapter delves deeper into the art of cementing influence and building lasting connections.

11.1. Understanding the Power of Connection

The journey starts with understanding the power of connection. Connection is the bedrock on which relationships are formed; it's where shared understanding, empathy, and trust flourish. In communication, connection acts as a bridge between individuals, helping them to comprehend and adapt to each other's perspectives. It's crucial for creating a conducive environment for fruitful dialogue and plays a pivotal role in fostering collaboration. Remember, the essence of connection is not to change or manipulate, but to understand and enable.

11.2. Building Trust: The Foundation of Connection

Trust is the foundation of every successful connection. It is an integral element of effective communication, without which there can be no genuine influence. Trust paves the way for openness and vulnerability, facilitating an atmosphere of mutual respect and understanding. It's built on consistent communication, promises kept, and actions that consistently align with words.

Effective communicators pay attention to their words and deeds, ensuring that they are not just trustworthy in their eyes, but also in the perspectives of others.

11.3. Emotional Intelligence: The Key to Influential Communication

Emotional Intelligence (EI) plays a key role in influential communication. Comprising dimensions like self-awareness, self-regulation, motivation, empathy, and social skills, EI empowers individuals to recognise, manage and respond to their own and others' emotions effectively.

An emotionally intelligent communicator understands the importance of listening, appreciating others' viewpoints, and responding appropriately. They are adept at connecting with others on a deeper level, making their conversations more authentic and impactful. We're in an age where the importance of EI can't be overstated for leveraging influence effectively.

11.4. Leveraging Persuasion and Inspiration

Persuasion and inspiration are among the most powerful tools in the influencer's kit. Persuasion is a technique of convincing or influencing others through credible communication. Make sure your argument is strong, logical, backed by facts, and most importantly, aligns with the interests of your audience.

Unlike persuasion, inspiration doesn't rely on arguments or

convincing. Instead, it's about sparking enthusiasm, stirring emotions, and igniting the inner drive of individuals. Effective communicators know the art of balancing persuasion with inspiration in their communication style.

11.5. Building Authenticity

Today's world values authenticity very highly. Your ability to be genuine and show up as you really are can significantly enhance your influence in communication. Acting with integrity, honouring your commitments, showing vulnerability when necessary, expressing gratitude, and admitting when you're wrong are all indicative of authenticity. They show that you're trustworthy and reliable, and people are more likely to be influenced by someone real rather than a perfect façade.

11.6. Consistent Messaging: From One to Many

Lastly, the relevance of consistent messaging can't be overstated. Regardless of the channel, the medium, or the audience, your message should remain coherent and consistent. This rule applies from one-to-one conversations to communicating to a large community or even your entire organisation. Inconsistencies can breed confusion and doubt, which are poison to influence.

In conclusion, remember that influence is a result of mindful practice and patience and is built on the foundations of trust, connection, and authentic, consistent communication. As we journey through the digital age, ensuring these principles are at the heart of all our interactions will not only help us become more effective communicators but also build richer, deeper, and more meaningful connections.